Crossing Jordan

Clues for Conquerors

By

Sam Darby

Karynn Press
PO Box 241
Douglassville, PA 19518
www.KarynnPress.com
SamDarby@DeJazzd.com

ISBN 978-0-578-02651-0

Cover Design by Sprint Art
Interior Design by Susan Reed
Copyediting by Book Babe

First published by Karynn Press June 8, 2009
Printed in the United States of America
Douglassville, PA

This book is printed on acid free paper.

To Sam and Jayne who opened the door, and
Walter, Elizabeth and Iris who kept a foot in it,
and Diane who helps me go through it and
Kelly and Sheldon and Krystal who are making
their own way through and Darby who will kick
the door wide open

Table of Contents

Introduction

"And all these things happened for examples: and they are written for our admonition, for us upon whom the ends of the world are come."
1 Corinthians 10:11

"The way to the Promised Land is through the wilderness."
Bruce Wilkinson

It's probably late summer. The year is 1490 BC. The Israelites stand on the brink of expectation. The God that led them from Egypt in a miraculous fashion, Who fed them and sustained them in the wilderness, is now inviting them to receive the object of their travail, the Promised Land. Spies have returned with reports of beauty, bounty and splendor. The descriptions enraptured the desert pilgrims with awe. But the spies also indicated that the land was filled with great walled cities which were populated by giants such as they had never seen. The majority report was that the land beyond Jordan, though desired, could not be inhabited due to the giants in the land and their impregnable walled cities.

Two of the twelve spies dissented. Their minority report asserted that the God Who brought them out of Egypt did not bring them through the desert to dwell on the west side of Jordan. If He could part the Red Sea, feed them in the desert, provide water from rock and maintain a cloud of protection about them, He most certainly could defeat the giants beyond Jordan.

Frequently we have the opportunity to make decisions upon which hang the nexus of destiny. The challenge is to recognize the situation and make the best choice. Our fear is that we will choose the wrong path and spend the rest of our lives ruing the decision. Israel was in that position. The no-brainer response should have been to accept the direction of the One Who had directed them out of Egypt and through the Red Sea.

The Israelites fear and/or lack of faith interrupted their crossing Jordan. They decided just a little too late that the path God directed was the better one and as a result they received a bonus of forty extra years to wander the wilderness before they would get another opportunity to traverse that river. An additional consequence of their action or lack there of was that all of the adults died in the process without ever entering the Promised Land. The only exceptions were the two faithful spies, the minority reporters Caleb and Joshua.

We come to Jordan Rivers in our lives. These are places and times where or when we have expectation and desire, but for some reason our actions just don't measure up. We want the Promised Land, but we don't want to cross Jordan to get there. It may be our fear of "giants" or their unassailable "walled cities." For some reason or another, the challenge of crossing Jordan creates such a block for us that we lose our desire for the beauty, bounty and splendor that lay beyond.

Could there be some valid reasons for staying on

the west side? Some might be satisfied with life as it is without crossing. Crossing might not be in their comfort zone. After all, there are giants over there. "Things are good," they say, "Why rock the boat?" When they contrast the security of what is known to the unpredictability of the unknown the former always wins. The resultant life is one that is not tried, not stretched and not challenged, but exists safely on the familiar banks of the river of unrealized potential.

God wanted Israel to accept His challenge for a quest of faith. Caleb and Joshua realized the prospective for adventure, for reward and for growth. Is there any place which is more exciting than being on the brink of the miraculous, led by Omnipotence to perform far beyond what we can ask or think?

Caleb and Joshua had been there, experiencing the rush and awe of seeing God at work. The ten plagues in Egypt, the breathtaking walk through the Red Sea, eating manna from heaven, and seeing water come gushing from a stone; they considered these but precursors of what God could and would do for them. You might say that they had an addiction for Omnipotence and they desired to cross Jordan just to see the miraculous.

There is a Jordan for you to cross. It's the challenge that besets your progress to meeting your goals. It's the thing that is outside of your comfort zone. But the lack is making a negative impression on your life. It might be affecting your relationships, or finances, or career or your ministry. Whatever it is, Christ has claimed the victory for you. Paul says that in Christ we are more than victors. What is lacking is the faith and the will to cross our Jordan and claim our victory.

This book is intended to firm our resolve, heighten our awareness to obstacles we create that diminish our ability to cross our Jordans, and to encourage our Christian growth. May you be blessed. I'll see you on the other side.

"To get something you never had, you must do something you have never done."

Chapter 1
What We Don't Know That We Don't Know

"There is a way that seemeth right unto a man,
but the ways thereof are the ways of death."
Proverbs 14:12

"No one wants advice, only corroboration"
John Steinbeck

"It is unwise to be sure of one's own wisdom. It is
healthy to be reminded that the strongest might weaken
and the strongest might err."
Mahatma Ganhdi

"There is no fool so great as a knowing fool"
Charles Haddon Spurgeon

A fatal flaw in our ability to cross Jordan is our fund of knowledge. We are wise beyond our years. The digital society maintains a depository of daunting data that can be accessed by merely googling or querying ask.com or Wikipedia (perish the thought). Because of televisions and satellites streaming images across the globe, we can safely say that we have surely seen it all. All of this awareness does not leave the possibility that there could be something, anything that has not been explored, tasted or documented. But yet there is. And the problem is that we don't know what we don't know. And if we don't know it, how can its knowledge be attained?

The following illustration may explain. James wants to do something for his son, Jimmy. So he asks him what he would like to do. Jimmy tells his father that what he wants is some french-fries. So James takes little Jimmy to the local fast food franchise and they go to the counter. Instead of the regular size that Jimmy wanted, James super sizes the order. Jimmy is in bliss as they move from the counter to the seat. He barely finishes saying his blessing before he begins devouring those golden sticks.

James watches, pleased with the little world that he has created for his son. He decides to taste one of Jimmy's fries. As he reaches in, Jimmy suddenly circles his arms around his meal and says, "No, Daddy, these are mine."

James is shocked at his son's reaction. Has Jimmy forgotten that James is his provider? Does he fail to realize that James is 6'2" and weighs 220 pounds and despite whatever Jimmy is doing with his arms around those fries, he can take as many as he wants? Maybe Jimmy doesn't remember that just as James bought those fries, which he super sized on a personal whim, he can also buy Jimmy more fries than he can ever eat.

The point is that God buys us fries every day. Unfortunately our response to His beneficence is too frequently the same as Jimmy's. And that's also the reason too many of us are on the wrong side of Jordan. We think we know, but we don't know what we need to know to cross our Jordan. Jimmy is holding on to his french-fries because he saw them as being crucial to any success that he might aspire to. In very much the same way, we have french-fries that prevent our own success.

I should be clear here. French-fries are symbolic for the things we feel will supplant the power of God as agents in our goal directed behavior. In no way is this discourse on healthy eating. The last thing that you should assume from any of this is that you should not eat french-fries. Although it may be a worthwhile admonition, it is not the intent of this writing. More to the point, let's look at why Jimmy looked to the french-fries rather than to his provider.

There is a reason why Jimmy didn't want to share his french-fries. What is it about french-fries that made Jimmy want to horde and not share? What is the lesson that we can learn about Jimmy and french-fries that will assist us in crossing?

Jimmy's issue was very simple. He placed more trust is the fries than he did in his father. Somehow he forgot his provider and only recognized his provision. In a way he is like the idol worshipper who carves an image out of stone and worships the creation rather than the creator.

Similarly we are like that when we place our trust in the gifts God has given us rather than the Giver. We trust in our cell phones, or bank accounts, lines of credit, the security of our jobs and of course our credit cards. What's the slogan? "Don't leave home without it." But how many of us won't leave home without prayer?

We put our trust in labels and name brands. I know people and you probably do also that refuse to wear any off brand label. I appreciate quality just like the next person. But I wonder if they are aware of how much free advertising they are giving every time they get dressed. Tommy, Nike, Versace, Nautica, Timberland, and Aeropostle are just some of the labels people seek.

A further irony exists in the fact that none of these labels or name brands is of any value in your quest to cross Jordan. As beautiful as they are they are not much more than rags when compared to the excellence of glory, which is given freely and without expense. That's totally different from the free gifts offers that I have seen when I shop. In order to get the gift, I have to make a purchase. My guess is that the price of the purchased item was adjusted to compensate for the free gift. Apparently the item in question is neither a gift nor free.

CDL

Nicci, Gucci and Christian Dior
Serucci and Pucci and plenty more
Cardin and Klein, Ainger and Beene
YSL on everything from sweaters to jeans
IZOD has the gator, playboy has the hare
There are emblems on everything, even underwear
But here are three letters CDL you see
It's a Christ designed life and the cost is free
CDL is from heaven and this is true
Christ had it first and he'll give it to you
It's been designed by the Master with a tailored

touch
Christ wants you to have it because he loves you so much
So why spend your money on what is not bread
Get the CDL look and you'll be way ahead.

I have to be honest. The first name I look for when I shop is Claire Hence. You know, Claire Hence Rack.

Are you starting to understand why Jimmy didn't want to give up the french-fries? They gave him security, although falsely based. Jimmy didn't know what he didn't know, that security is in the Giver and not in the gift. The result is that Jimmy and all of us like him will remain on the west side of Jordan.

What gives you your sense of security? Is it riches? It's nice to have a secure financial future, to have enough money that money is not the issue. It's good to have money. People say money talks. So I ask them what it says and most people tell me it says, "Goodbye!" They tell me they have to take their check to the bank because it's too small to go by itself. Most of the decisions we make on a daily basis are based on money. The story is told of a young millionaire who was considering the idea of a pre-nuptial agreement. He asked his fiancée if she would still love him if he were broke. Her answer was, "Of course I'd still love you, but I would miss you terribly!" The rich young ruler went away sorrowfully because he had much money. Too many individuals have broken relationships, lied and even murdered because of money.

And rightfully spoken it is the love of money that is

the root of all evil. Money, however, never performed a crime, nor will it ever. It is our fixation on the gift rather than what the Giver intended. I am not saying that you shouldn't have money. We need it for everything we do. What happens though is when we forget Who gave it to us, when we focus more on it than heaven, when we cannot return a faithful tithe and offering, we're just like Jimmy and the french-fries.

Proverbs 23.5

"Wilt thou set thine eyes upon that which is not? For riches certainly make themselves wings; they fly away as an eagle toward heaven."

Riches provide a temporal security; for those of us wanting to live in an eternal society it is not enough. For those of us desiring to cross Jordan it is insufficient. Placing our confidence in riches is the same as Jimmy's obsession with his french-fries.

Maybe this illustration can place riches in the perspective of eternity. Imagine that you have a little child, let's make it an infant 3-4 months old. To get her attention you take a shiny ornament, something cheap but gaudy. The child is instantly transfixed by its apparent opulence to the point that if you were to attempt to exchange the orb for a $10 bill, the baby would burst into outrage. The outrage occurred due to the fact that the tot didn't know what she didn't know. God sees earthly riches as nothing but that child's toy, to amuse and bring pleasure but in no way to satisfy. Unfortunately we are too often caught at the identical level of development as the child as it relates to seeing the eternal picture. The baby cannot perceive that anything could be more satisfying than the bauble. In the same way we are so obsessed with the power of money that we are unable to acknowledge the Creator of all. At some point children mature and learn the value of money (so to speak), God wishes to improve the learning curve in our understanding of eternal values.

We could go on and on about money. Christ, in fact spent a lot of time talking about money and our relationship to it. But there are some other things on which we place french-fry like trust, things that will keep us all citizens of the west side.

I am pleased with my accomplishments, my degrees and certifications, my CDs that I've published, my website, the books I have written etc. But it becomes french-fries once I value it over my relationship with Christ, once I feel that it was accomplished on my power, once I use it as a reason to say that I am better than anyone else or dishonor my Creator.

James 4.14
"What is your life? Is it even a vapor, that appeareth for a little while and then vanisheth away?"

1 Peter 2.4
"For all flesh is grass and all the glory of man is as the flower of grass. The grass withereth and the flower fadeth away."

What both of these texts are saying is that if we trust in french-fries we will disappear like a Happy Meal in the back seat of a van. But somehow we think that our fries are special. And we say things or act in a way that says: Because I'm a high school senior, or a senior citizen, or a Christian, or not a Christian, or a PhD or a high school drop out, or I'm married, or I'm single, or I make a 6 figure salary or I am unemployed, that you need to treat me a certain way. The rules are different for me because of my unique situation. And we trust in our claim to fame rather than in Jesus' name.

You think because he's young and beautiful that he doesn't have an STD. You think because you are in the church you won't be tempted to sin. Just because you are a deacon or an elder doesn't make you exempt. Your title means nothing when the hot breath of a salacious liaison beacons you to infidelity. Your GPA or your portfolio won't prevent you from losing your mind when a friend tells you to try it, you'll like it. Fifty years of sitting in the pew will mean nothing to a soul consumed in selfishness, bitterness and inflexibility. And all of these will keep you watching the water from the wrong side.

Proverbs 28:26 –
He that trusteth in his own heart is a fool.

By placing trust in yourself all you are doing is filling up your cup for the day of reckoning. And when it's full the only question I have for you is this: Do you want fries with that?

I could talk about the other things to which we transfer the trust that we should place in God. For example there's beauty. Looks fade. God's word lasts. There is physical strength. It doesn't last. Some athletes have even risked their careers and even their lives by taking performance-enhancing drugs in order to get a few moments of fame. It should be remembered that fame and the adulation of fans are fleeting. Just remember this, the same crowd that said, "Hosanna" also said, "Crucify Him."

What about men's promises? My mother always told me to get it in writing. That's reasonable advice. Unfortunately many promises are no better than the paper that they were written on. If you don't believe me, check with any Native American. And if the contract is to be accepted there is still so much small print that the pact itself has little power.

Education, jobs, friends, our retirement plan, even our spouses – at the very best they are all uncertainties. I've seen people with PhDs mopping floors, secure jobs pink slipped with 2 weeks notice, friends fail and spouses become unfaithful.

Brothers and sisters we need to base our lives on something sturdier than what feels good, what tastes good, what looks good, or what is in our comfort zone. Unless we do that we are no better than the Israelites creating a golden calf. Why? Because we have made an image and we are worshipping it. We have replaced the power of God Almighty for the security of an uncertainty. We have erected a temple and placed self on its pedestal. And we have no more power to save our souls than did Baal or Ashtoreth, or Vin Diesel or Jet Li or Alycia Keys or 50 Cent.

God's appeal to us is to accept the only one sure word of prophecy based on promises that never fail.

1 Kings 8:56 –

Blessed be the Lord, that hath given rest unto His people Israel, according to all that he promised: there hath not failed one word of all his good promise. Not one unfailing promises – no small print – all of His promises are good.

Isaiah 28.16 –

Therefore thus saith the Lord God, "Behold I lay in Zion for a foundation a stone. A tried stone, a precious cornerstone, a sure foundation…"

On what do you want to base your eternity, a foundation stone or a french-fry? Or would your french-fry be more desirable if it were super sized?

God wants us despite our wanton desire for all things unholy, despite our willful ignorance, despite our west side of Jordan mentality. Romans 8:38 says, "I am persuaded, that neither death, nor life, nor angels, nor principalities, nor angels, nor powers nor things present, nor things to come, nor height, nor depth, nor any creature shall be able to separate us from the love of God, which is in Christ Jesus our Lord."

If an all-powerful God wants nothing to separate us, can anything come in between? As strange as it may seem the answer to that question is yes. God in His love has given you the power to over rule His design. But He's also given you the power to choose eternal life and it's as easy as requesting a happy meal.

Brothers and sisters, God wants you to accept his offer and go nuts. NUTS is an acronym, where the letters stand for never underestimate the Spirit. Just think what type of spiritual life, what type of relations, what type of finances, what type of influence, what type of witness, what type of ministry you would have if you existed in a place of optimum expectancy based on the Holy Spirit.

Unfortunately the popular trend is to trust in "french-fries" rather than in the power of the Holy Ghost. Your need for "french-fries" diminishes as you move into a faith relationship with God. And He promises to do exceedingly abundantly more than we can ask or think.

What can God do through you right where you are? Are you being fully utilized by the Spirit or could you start a new ministry? Why don't you begin with something your community needs more than anything else? Here is how you can determine just what it is. It's the thing that everyone has a dozen reasons for as to why it can't be done. You will hear experts on the subject rehearse how many times it was attempted and give chapter and verse as to why, though it is needed, you shouldn't waste your time. Don't you know that we serve the God of the impossible? Do we believe God can do it or do we limit the Spirit?

Maybe it is a combination of ignorance and arrogance. We have deluded ourselves as to the potency of our "french-fries" so that we take it personally when they are challenged. We will concoct reasons or excuses to defend our "fries." I believe in the maxim that you can make excuses or you can make progress, but you cannot make both. The self-deluded and the excuse makers have a good time together. However, you will never see them on the east side of Jordan.

I was recently talking with a church group about expanding their ministry. They gave me several reasons why it wouldn't work; poor community image, everything has been tried before without any success, and they didn't feel that the locals would respond well to their message. All those reasons are "french-fries." They don't know what they don't know.

I had a similar conversation with a principal of a Christian school about the need to expand. He agreed that it was necessary, but he said that it would have to wait because the church that supported the school was involved in other financially consuming projects at the time. "French-fries again," I say. Though well intentioned, that principal did not know what he did not know. In both cases ignorance of the will of God and the power of God kept them and their ministry stranded on the wrong side of Jordan.

We do not succeed or fail any venture because of our plans. Our success and failure depend on our relationship to His plan. Building a new school is a daunting task. Expanding your church's ministry is equally intimidating. Crossing your Jordan may be just as threatening. But if we can expect to do it ourselves, why do we need God? If there is no need for a miracle, why do we need

God? If I can handle it with my "french-fries," why do I need God? So my advice to them was to build the new school and baptize 50 new members. They said, "You're nuts!" I said, "I hope so!" I don't ever want to exist anywhere that is outside the power of the miraculous.

Brothers and sisters we need to go nuts
Get to action & off your you-know-whats
The power of God is more than enough
Brothers and sisters we need to go nuts

The signs say the time of end is close
We need the power of the Holy Ghost
To give the world what they need the most
The love of God in a double dose

Some say things are not so bad
They have more money than they ever had
But the current lifestyle is just a fad
Put treasure in heaven & you'll be glad

Learn to walk by faith not sight
One road's broad and the other tight
Trust the path that leads to the light
Your reward in heaven is out a sight

Brothers and sisters we got to go nuts
Get to action & off your you-know-whats
The power of God is more than enough
Brothers and sisters we've got to go nuts

The difference between west side residents and east side residents, between crossers and non-crossers is the capacity for going nuts. That is the ability to move by faith alone and grab hold of the Unseen to do the impossible.

There is a poem by Apollinaire that goes like this:

Come to the edge
You'll push us
Come to the edge
We're afraid
Come to the edge
And he pushed them
And they flew

Do you want to fly, fly higher than the highest human thought? Do you want to cross Jordan? Lose the french-fries, and I'll meet you on the other side.

Chapter 2

In the Belly of the Beast

They that observe lying vanities
forsake their own mercy.
Jonah 2:8

"When you rationalize, you tell rational lies."
Sam Darby

"I was not lying, I just said things that later on seemed
to be untrue."
Richard Nixon

Enter the world of Rocko and Heft, a raccoon and cow created on the cels of anime for the purpose of our amusement and delight. In this particular episode, Rocko was cleaning his house when Heft came to visit. It was obvious that Heft's visit was ill timed and that Rocko was consumed with the busyness of household maintenance. Heft decided to help by sitting on the couch and watching television.

You can imagine the scene; Rocko cleaning, vacuuming and dusting while Heft is surfing through the channels via the remote control. Suddenly Rocko's vacuum emits a window-rattling screech, discharges a cloud of dust and dies on the spot. And wouldn't you just know it? At that moment a commercial for vacuum cleaners is on TV. Rocko and Heft are instantly impressed and call the number on the screen. Instantly the doorbell rings and the vacuum is delivered in typical cartoon fashion. Rocko unpacks it, plugs it in and gets it going. He starts vacuuming again. This machine is some type of super vacuum because it starts sucking up everything. It not only picks up dirt, it also picks up the clothes from the floor; it picks up the rug, the couch, and the television. Rocko loses control to the point that he and Heft are ultimately consumed by this super appliance. The final scene shows them comfortably going on with their life inside the vacuum cleaner.

They are inside the belly of the beast. That does sound ominous, but they were in a situation of their own construction, obliviously ignorant of their peril, continuing life as usual in the belly of the beast. They were cut off from the real world, in the belly of the beast. They were separated from reality, living a life that is a sham and a farce. They were cut off from truth, living in a virtual reality, in the belly of the beast.

This phenomenon is not the sole domain of toons and fictional characters. I would suspect that there are many people who are actually alive whose lives are locked in neutral, whose days are busy but not fulfilling, who speak loudly, but say nothing, who are caught up in a world that has no meaning or future. They are sitting right beside Rocko and Heft in the belly of the beast. They have become so obsessed with living that they don't have time for life. They have become so consumed with the day-to-day pressures that they have forgotten their purpose, their calling, and the reason for their creation. They say, "I'll do it, I'll get to it. Right now I'm busy."

But it never gets done. The mundane has consumed their passion. They are in the belly of the beast, caught up in their own world.

If anyone would know about being in the belly of the beast it is Jonah. Jonah was caught up in his own world and in the second Chapter of Jonah we find his prayer from the belly of the beast. A look at his prayer reveals his understanding as to why he is where he is. Notice verse 8, "They that observe lying vanities forsake their own mercy." These lying vanities are idols. Jonah wasn't an idol worshipper, but he was familiar with lying vanities. Lying vanities are more than graven images or idols. These vanities are the thoughts that lead us away from the truth. They are the ways we placate ourselves to keep our conscious quiet when we know we aren't doing what we are supposed to be doing.

It is not a secret that sin begins in the mind. Unfortunately we focus more on the sinful deed than the thought that inspired it. When someone curses or unfairly berates someone and they feel uncomfortable about it, they usually apologize by saying something like "it just slipped out." The fact is that if it weren't in there to begin with, there would be no need to worry about it slipping out. The WWJD (What Would Jesus Do?) slogan places focus more on the act than the thought that inspires it. It is the thought that precedes the action. Adam's sin followed Adam's thought. Your sin is followed by your thought. We are told that if we hate our brother (or sister) it is the same as murder. If we look leeringly at a man or woman it is the same as adultery. Since sin begins in the mind, a more appropriate and provocative slogan would be WWJT. That is; What Would Jesus Think?

Lying vanities are things like rationalization, denial, reaction formation, projection and avoidance. We called them defense mechanisms in Psychology 101. We use these thought processes to insulate ourselves from things that are painful. Insulation from pain is good. It becomes problematic when the insulation distorts reality or inhibits the growth of character. Mature mechanisms like humor, altruism, sublimation, and suppression facilitate growth and when you use them you don't have to end up in the belly of the beast or on the wrong side of Jordan.

Avoidance

Jonah used avoidance when he ran away from God's command. He thought that he could solve the problem by running away from it. But running away gave him more problems. Life is about solving problems. When we avoid issues we just delay the resolution. The matter will resurface and resurface each time more ominous than before until we address it. But people think, like Jonah that if they can avoid it long enough it will go away. So they run away from school, from jobs, from relationships, from marriages and from responsibilities only to see that same problem appear again and again until it is adequately addressed.

Addressing the problem gives an opportunity for

growth. For example, most children are fearful of the dark. Carrying that fear into adulthood could be problematic. One mother realized that when she asked her young son to go out on the porch in the dark and retrieve her broom. She saw that he was hesitant because he was afraid of the dark. Sensitive to her son's needs, she wanted to assist him in conquering his fear of the dark. So she told him that he should not be afraid because Jesus is everywhere. Evidently he wasn't quite ready to take that leap into the dark so he replied to his mother, "Then maybe we could ask Jesus to get the broom."

Life is full of problems. Successful people, Jordan crossers, accept these ground rules without demur. The key to success is to be able to select the problem that you wish to have. For example you want a car so that you can drive to work. The purchase of a car solves the problem of transportation, but it creates another problem of car maintenance, insurance, registration and etcetera. Some have decided that car ownership is more problematic than public transportation. As a result they don't own a car. What they have done is to select the problem with which they choose to live and operate out of that paradigm. It's like the story about the man who had a cold and went to his physician for healing. The doctor told him to sit outside in frigid weather with no clothes on. The patient protested, saying that it was ridiculous and that he would get pneumonia. The doctor agreed with his patient's prognosis. He then gave clarity to his prescription. The physician explained that he had made that recommendation because he knew how to cure pneumonia but not a cold.

As we mature we are expected to be less avoidant. Meeting problems head on is a sign of maturity. It is definitely a quality of Jordan crossers. The Israeli host wished so desperately to avoid the conflict that would validate their ownership of the Promised Land that the Lord gave them what they wanted. They avoided both the conflict and the conquest. Every success has its price, as does every avoidant behavior. You can't have a crown without a cross. There is no testimony without a test. There is no Promised Land without a wilderness. There is no reward without crossing Jordan. West side residents avoid the challenge and thus have no opportunity to gain the winner's prize.

Denial

Jonah was in denial (actually it was somewhere in the Mediterranean Sea). That is a dangerous place to be especially in relation to God. Jonah denied reality. He actually thought that he could run away from God. To think that you can run away from God means that you can go somewhere that God doesn't know about. Would that mean that you know more than God? Interesting, isn't it? That's why Jonah was in denial.

We deny God's power by limiting His influence in our lives. We deny His wisdom by choosing our way over His. We deny our need for a Savior by worshipping at the feet of secular theology and humanism. We deny the special ness of our calling by immersing our-selves into the world to the extent that the peculiarity for which we are noted (God says we are to be His peculiar people) can be barely distinguished.

We are the church of Laodicea that the Holy One appeals to in Revelation. (Revelation 3: 14-22) They are the poster children for denial. They say they are rich and increased with goods. Western society has more trash than the third world has food. They say they have need of nothing. Do you have trouble buying gifts for people, because you can't think of anything to give them because they have everything? So you end up buying them something else that they don't need and the cycle of excess is perpetuated. The telling part of the passage is this, "Don't you know that you are poor and miserable and blind and naked." Is that not the height of denial?

Now it is one thing to walk around with spinach in your teeth. It is another thing to stroll through a restaurant with toilet paper stuck to your shoe or even with a zipper open. It is an entirely different matter to be naked and not only unaware of your nakedness, but operating under the assumption that you are attired in the most current trend setting togs.

But that's Laodicea's predicament. Every soul who assumes righteousness outside of God's purview is in the same predicament. God interprets our efforts at self-righteousness as filthy rags. You can deny it as much as you like, it won't change your status. Wake up and smell that morning beverage of choice and realize exactly what your reality is.

In addition to denying the power of God, people in denial also deny their responsibility. Lawsuits abound as a result of people denying personal culpability and surrendering their power of choice to convenient circumstance. A burglar who injured his leg during a robbery sued the homeowner. Another bank robber sued the lending institution that he held up because the money that he had stolen had an explosive dye concealed within. When it unexpectedly went off in his pocket and damaged some of his personal items, he felt compelled to sue. It is not the tobacco company's fault that I chose to smoke their addictive and debilitating product and developed a fatal diagnosis. It is not McDonald's fault that I don't know that I shouldn't try to operate an automobile with a boiling cup of coffee between my knees. If I want the freedom to choose, I need to be able to accept the results of my choice. To his credit, Jonah got this one right. The account says he took responsibility for the storm that threatened the ship he was in. Jordan crossers get it. Everyone else is looking for a lawyer.

Our actions have a broader culpability than just ourselves. When was about six or seven years old I was given the opportunity to plant a flower garden in the yard. This was a grand privilege beyond anything I had undertaken in my brief existence. I could select the flowers, plant, water and weed. I remember going with my mother to the store to choose the seed pack. The one that caught my imagination was the zinnia. The picture on the pack was dramatic and the name had a little zip to it.

I prepared the plot and followed the directions on

the pack for planting. I carefully packed the soil around each seed while vision of blooms danced in my head. I watered and waited. My mother told me that is would take some time. So each day I watered and waited. One day I noticed green sprigs pushing their way through the dirt. My zinnias were on their way.

As they grew taller, my mother observed that my plants were not zinnias. In fact, she told me that they were weeds. Then she said the impossible. She told me to cut them out! I ran a gamut of feelings from shock to distrust to denial. These little plants were my plants. There is no way I could grow anything but zinnias. Regardless of what my mother said, they would not be weeds. I would not let that happen. I would show her just how much she knew. She would see my beautiful blossoms and apologize for ever casting aspersions on the quality of my garden's output. It was with a clear conscious that I disobeyed her directive and I did not do anything to my blooms-to-be but continue to care for them.

A few days later, my mother chastised me for not cutting out the "weeds". And if further evidence was needed she showed me thorns growing on my "zinnias." I pled for a few more days reprieve for the threatened flowers on the basis that roses have thorns also. The possibility for a unique breed of blossom was imminent. The buds were in evidence and their opening appeared to be soon.

The blooms I anticipated never appeared. Instead, thistles took their place. As they blew throughout the yard, depositing seed after seed, I was reminded of my mother's warning and direction. As I spent the summer ridding the yard of my "zinnias" I gained a better understanding of not only how I am affected by denial, but of the effect my denial has on my environment.

Projection

This lying vanity labels others with our own traits. For example, Jonah did not want to preach to the Ninevites because he thought that they would not accept the truth. The reason that he thought that was because he was the one who had problems with the truth. Why else did he try to run from God? Rather than addressing his issues, he projected his weaknesses upon the Ninevites.

Generally the traits we are the first to identify are the ones we know the most about. You've heard the expression, "Takes one to know one." Is it not the gossip that accuses others of gossiping or the thief that alarms against stealing? Prevaricators can usually tell when someone is lying.

The problem with this defense mechanism is that the perpetrator appears to be guiltless. In fact they are seen as a watchman or some type of social police indicating society's misfits. The perception is erroneous. The pariah they caution is closer than they think. As Pogo said, "We have met the enemy and he is us."

East side residents who employ the lying vanity of projection will be the first to criticize someone for not being bold enough to attempt to cross Jordan. Actually they are critical of anyone who tries to better themselves. They are like the disciples in the boat who teased Peter about walking on the water, when they were unable to get out of the boat themselves.

Rationalization

Jonah used logic to excuse his behavior. He actually thought that he could escape God by jumping overboard. We think we can escape God's judgment, too. We say, "God won't send me to hell because I curse a little." Or we might say, "God loves me too much to let me burn because I don't tithe." That's why when we rationalize, we tell rational lies. God does love you. It is true that He doesn't want you to burn in hell. It is true that there is a Heaven that He wishes for you. In fact it is true that there will be people in heaven who cursed, stole, fornicated and even did not return their tithe.

Here is where the rationalization breaks down. There is a hell and there will be people there who cursed, stole, fornicated and held their tithe. The issue of salvation is not God's choice. He has already made His choice. It is a matter of your choice. If you choose God over cursing, stealing, fornicating and keeping your tithe, there is an eternity waiting. If you select profanity, theft, whore-mongering and theft again (that's what keeping your tithe is), the best asbestos suit won't help you no matter how you try to rationalize your way out of it.

These lying vanities brought Jonah to the belly of the beast. The account says that he was there for three days

35

and nights. I wonder what he was thinking about. My guess is that he began processing his thought patterns that got him where he was. He had hit bottom and he needed to look up. Einstein suggested that if you want different results than what you have then you have to use a different kind of thinking than you used to create your situation. If you are stuck on the wrong side of Jordan, you need to change the way you have been thinking.

That can be a tricky assignment, especially if you are on the wrong side of Jordan. One of the first things people will do is ask advice, which is a good thing. The problem is whom they ask for advice. If you are on the wrong side of Jordan, the people that you will engage are in the same circumstance as you are. They are probably the least likely to give any useful advice. Anything they tell you is highly suspect. They don't have the experience, or knowledge, or frame of reference to be of any use. It is not that they are bad people they just can't help you.

It took Jonah three days and three nights of talking to the whale to realize the same thing. The whale couldn't give any advice. He and Jonah shared predicaments. And so, stuck in the belly of the beast, Jonah looked up and spoke up and prayed up to a God that he had been using his best reasons to get away from. In his moment of conviction he vowed to avoid the lying vanities. He demonstrated a change in thought that would initiate a change in action.

The lying vanities have kept many a pilgrim stranded on the west side of Jordan. Puffed up in their self-righteousness they have a plethora of rationalities as to why they are victims and not victorious. If you listen to them long enough, you will find sufficient excuse yourself. Reject the lying vanities and their addictive allure and I'll see you on the other side.

Chapter 3
Stinking Thinking

"A merry doeth good like a medicine: but a broken
spirit drieth the bones."
Proverbs 17:22

"If you can't say anything nice, don't say anything at all."
Your Mother

As a man thinketh in his heart, so is he.
Solomon

This single topic has more potency for potential impact in your personal life than probably any other. Throughout our lives, we can point to people who have been a positive influence on us. We can probably remember the ones that had a negative influence also. They were usually the ones your mother told you to avoid. She was afraid that their negative influence would be detrimental. She thought it would rub off on you and virtually prevent your possibilities for prosperity. You can most likely remember people who called you names, teased you or otherwise ruined your day by some type of negative behavior.

What is most interesting is that the preponderance of perpetrators of anti-positive behavior practice practically without punishment. The reason why we are so easy on them is that we are those perpetrators. We are the guilty ones. It begins in our thought life. We think on average about 10,000 thoughts a day. For most of us, only about thirteen percent of those thoughts are positive. Throughout the day we are bombarding ourselves with more negative messages than the town bully, that overbearing supervisor and that driver that you cut off combined.

We tell ourselves that we are incapable, unlovable, and invisible. And we add to that a host of other diminutives. If anyone else told us those things we would become instantly defensive, sever all personal relationships and take their names off our Christmas card list. Yet this is the way we live, uncertain, paranoid and constantly defensive, lest anyone should see past our veneer of self-assuredness and realize the wretched inadequate people that we really sense we are.

If your assessment of yourself were accurate, then your behavior would be justified. However, the assessment I have just described is an opinion, your opinion of yourself. Opinions are not right or wrong. They are opinions. They are neither fact nor fantasy. They are opinions. They can fluctuate just like the weather depending upon internal and external stimuli. Imagine this, you leave the barbershop or styling salon with what you think is a pretty lousy haircut. The stylist blew it, in your opinion. But on the way home, total strangers, who seem pretty normal, stop you and each of them complements your new coif. I guarantee you that somewhere between the tonsorial parlor and your abode you opinion of your haircut will change. Your haircut didn't change, just your opinion of it. Have you ever asked someone how they like the weather and on the same day you can get an equal number of favorable and unfavorable responses? Did the weather change? The responses were all opinions. So here's the magic secret. If you can decide what type of opinion to have, why not have a positive one? If you are going to have an opinion of yourself, why not make it a good one?

Being positive or negative is a choice. Why not choose those thought patterns that are beneficial as opposed to those that are detrimental? It is indeed a choice. I live by the creed that if I'm having a bad day it is nobody's fault but mine. If I am going to be upset, it is my choice. If I am elated, it is my choice. I am the arbitrator, the mediator, and the filter for every stimulus that comes my way. I am the judge, the umpire and the referee. I have the final word on how I will respond. It is a matter of personal election.

The rewards for a positive mental set are many. King Solomon writes in the book of Proverbs that a merry heart is like medicine, but a broken spirit dries the bones. He states further that a merry heart makes a happy countenance, but by sorrow of heart the spirit is broken.

These two proverbs establish the relationship between our mental state and our physical health. The best medicine is a positive attitude. You have seen it validated in your own experience. How often has a negative comment ruined your day? Modern science also verifies this. I have even heard some estimates as high as 90% of all illnesses are mentally induced. Most heart attacks occur on Mondays. Why do you think that is so? I think it is because so many people would rather not go to work on Monday. Something about the job they find disagreeable. That's a big price to pay for stinking thinking.

I remember when I was in college; I developed a significant pain in my lower abdomen. The fellows in the dorm decided that I should see the campus doctor. Several of the guys shared with me their diagnosis and prognosis of my ailment based on their experience. After listening to them, I became increasingly concerned about my future health because none of their outcomes seemed that positive. A friend helped me walk across campus to the doctor. I was not in good shape. My steps were measured to minimize the pain. It was all that I could do to fall into the seat in the waiting room. I felt as though the end was near. I envisioned my funeral. I wondered how my parents would take the news. After what seemed like an eternity, I was called to the examination room. The doctor examined me and gave me a prescription. He said I should be fine. It was a miracle, indeed, because I was fine. This doctor was a great healer. At his word my pain left and I returned with élan across the campus. Yes, I did have a physical ailment, but my stinking thinking made it so much worse.

The most infectious type of stinking thinking is worry. Worry debilitates. William Inge says that worry is interest paid on trouble before it falls due. For all of the energy it expends, it solves little. At its root is a lack of faith. It is actually an insult to God to worry. How can we worry when we serve an all-powerful God who loves us? Paul says whatever is not of faith is sin. Worry is not

41

of faith. Worry is sin. It is an easy trap to fall in. But it is not productive. It is not positive. It can rob you of your faith. And it can keep you stranded on the wrong side of Jordan.

My mother knew how to worry. She would worry if I were too fat. She would worry if I were too slim. She would worry that I would get to work safely and she would worry if I would get home on time. She would even tell me that she was afraid that she was worrying too much. And when she would ask me if I thought that she worried too much I was afraid to tell her yes because she would worry about it. Unfortunately, I inherited her worry gene. For years I would lie awake at nights running through scenarios, many of which never occurred. One day, the truth of Paul's text hit me like a stone and I prayed for victory over worry. And I must say since that time I haven't been worry free. I've had a few relapses, but overall I have just decided to let God handle those things I can't control, which is everything! I have gained nothing for all my years of worry. However since I've been on the worry-free program I have less stress and more peace of mind and I have improved my relationship with Christ.

Another effect of your affect is that like breeds like. People enjoy being around positive people. And the opposite is also true. Misery truly loves company. The lesson here is if you align yourself with positive people, you will reap the effects of their pro-social outlook. Conversely negative communication can only have a negative effect.

It is important to remember that whatever we give attention to, we expand. That is, the more attention we give to negative situations, the larger those things become. It is as though we are breathing energy into all of that bad stuff and giving it more life. This is why people become overwhelmed with their problems. Their attention to the negative (bad bosses, poor working conditions, weight problems, disobedient children, nagging parents or spouses, health issues, etc.) only makes the issues larger than life. As a practice it is vital to not respond to the need to rehearse your bad experiences. They will consume you and you will wonder why you can't get away from them. It is because you are constantly breathing life into them by your daily carping.

I need to mention that the kind of attention that I am referencing is not the solution-based attention, where people are problem solving. Rather it borders on a pity party type of focus. The participants here are only interested in airing their problems and discussing their unfortunate lot. And then they wonder why the problems never go anywhere. It is because they are exhausting themselves by breathing their own energy into the problems they wish would disappear. Ironic isn't it?

If the formula is true, (and it is) that whatever we give attention to we expand, then it would seem to be much more productive to choose to focus on the positive. We have demonstrated how this will improve the quality of your life physically, emotionally and socially.

It will also improve your spiritual life in at least a couple of ways. The opposite of complaining is praise.

My suggestion is to find a reason for praise when you wish to complain. What you will be doing is breathing life into the positive and extinguishing that which is negative. Additionally, David tells us in Psalm 22.3 that God inhabits the praise of His people. I take that to mean that you are able to create a personal tabernacle of praise in which God Almighty dwells just by choosing to praise rather than complain. That is something stinking thinking cannot accomplish even on a good day. It is all a matter of choice.

It will also improve your prayer life. Negativity, worry and doubt are not consistent with the prayer of faith. James 1.5-6 promises that God will give liberally if we ask in faith with nothing wavering. Verse 8 says a double minded man is unstable in all his ways. Several times throughout the Gospels Christ encourages us to ask. Matthew 7.21 says that whatever we ask in prayer believing, we shall receive.

A positive attitude, what the Bible calls faith, is key to a bountiful prayer life. God has an abundance of blessings to bestow upon His children. He wants us to believe and He encourages us to ask. Faith is the key by which we gain access to the promises of God.

Wayne Dyer in his book There is a Spiritual Solution to Every Problem describes how our focus can inhibit our spiritual relationships. The short version is that we operate in three levels of consciousness; ego-consciousness, group consciousness and God consciousness. The lowest level, ego-consciousness is characterized by fear, anxiety, and stress. You operate within a paradigm that separates you from everyone else and places you in competition with the world. Primary concerns are what you have, what you do and what others think of you. At this stage, Dyer asserts, individuals are as far away from the energy of God as possible.

Dyer believes that as people progress to average or normal consciousness they move up to the next level, group consciousness. Identity here is derived on the basis of what group you are from or have chosen to align yourself with. Us vs. them verbiage is typical of this stage. Wars and genetic cleansings are the responsibility of this level of consciousness. Pain and illness are accepted as the norm in this level.

Only as we move into the level of God consciousness are we able to actually bring healing to others and ourselves. God consciousness is the antithesis of stinking thinking. This is the paradigm of positive philosophy. You are at one with the Creator. The negativity that fosters the separateness and competition of ego-consciousness and group consciousness is absent. Your attitude is one of acceptance rather than criticism. Dyer characterizes your message to the universe as "no longer 'Gimme, gimme, gimme,' but, 'How can I give?'"

Very clearly a positive lifestyle begins and ends with our focus. It's a simple as a choice of seeing the glass as half empty or half full. Faith feeds the positive. Fear feeds the negative.

Doubt, worry and fear are the ways that our own stinking thinking can defeat us. Where doubt and worry might be learned, we are wired to have fear. It is a part of our defense system. Whenever our protection systems see us in a threat situation, fear signals the body and the natural reaction is to retreat until we are safe. This is quite appropriate when encountering a black bear in the wilderness, but probably less appropriate when facing a challenge that has growth potential.

Faith and fear, doubt and worry have all the same basic definition. They are all a belief in the unknown. They all spur reaction based on that belief, but the end results could not be more different. The question each of us must answer is whether we want our lives to be directed by fear or by faith. Do you want the bondage of doubt and worry? Clean up your stinking thinking and I'll see you on the other side.

Chapter 4
Streak for Jesus

"Let us lay aside every weight, and the sin that doeth so easily beset us and run with patience the race that is set before us."
Hebrews 12:1

"He ain't rude.
He's just in the mood to run in the nude."
Ray Stevens

"Fidelity to commitment in the face of doubts and fears is a really spiritual thing."
Real Live Preacher

Webster's dictionary defines streak as a transitive verb, meaning to run naked in a public place. Streaking hit a high level of popularity in the 70's. It was not so much a movement of nudism as it was of exhibitionism. According to one researcher the average streaker was a Protestant male undergraduate who weighed 170 lbs and maintained a B average. He hailed from a town with a population under 50,000. His father was a businessman and his mother a housewife. The female streakers, though much in the minority, average 5 foot 3 inches in height and weighed about 117 lbs.

Some viewed this movement as some type of non-violent protest. One young man darted through the state legislative chamber in Hawaii proclaiming himself the streaker of the house. Another exhibitionist streaked for the impeachment of President Nixon in Washington, DC.

But most just considered it a silly pastime. Ray Stevens captured the spirit in his song "The Streaker." The lyrics were, "He ain't rude, he's just in the mood to run in the nude." Streakers made their mark on any public gathering. Nothing was off limits, graduations, sporting events and even church services. The most famous streaking incident took place during the televised 1974 Academy Awards ceremony. David Niven was introducing Elizabeth Taylor when a naked runner disrupted the going ons.

When I moved to Trenton, NJ in the winter of '77 there was an account of a man seen running down West State Street, a main thoroughfare, with nothing but a ski cap on. Further investigation revealed (no pun intended) he wasn't really a streaker. He was caught trying to steal the wrong person's car. The owner of the car gave him the option of either accepting a bullet or running through the snow wearing just his cap and a smile.

Streaking is not confined to youthful runners. I was told of an eighty-year-old fellow who got inspired by all of these young chaps streaking and decided to streak past two elderly ladies living down the block. They were obviously shocked. Their conversation proceeded like this;
"Edna, did you see that?"
"Yes, what was that he had on?"
"I'm not sure, but it looked like it needed ironing."
Running naked is not a 70's phenomenon. The early

Olympic races were all completed in the nude. I think it made them be more careful.

So I guess you're wondering at this point where we are going with this. And it might seem a little ridiculous to you, but the title of this chapter is Streak for Jesus. Let's look in the Bible and see if we can find examples of how we can streak for Jesus and what streaking for Jesus has to do with crossing Jordan. I found three examples of streaking in the Bible. You might find more. But these are the ones we will consider.

The first is in Luke 8:26, 27.

And they arrived in the country of the Gadarenes, which is over against Galilee.
And when He went forth to land, there met Him our of the city a certain man, which had devils a long time, and ware no clothes, neither abode in any house, but in tombs."

You are familiar with the incident. A man filled with demons met Christ and his disciples. He ran toward them when they touched on shore. Obviously his appearance was unsettling to them to say the least. The devils that possessed him made him rage and kept him naked. In fact once the devils were removed we find him in verse 35 clothed and quiet.

This fellow streaked because he was full of the devil. There are a lot of things people do when they are full of the devil. And sometimes people feel the best solution is to beat the devil out of them. But in this case, once

49

he met the Savior, the devils left him and he stopped his streaking ways. His streaking was not an active choice. And he was obviously not streaking for Jesus. So we will move on to the next example found in Mark 14: 51 and 52.

And there followed Him a certain young man, having a linen cloth cast about his naked body; and the young men laid hold on him. And he left the linen cloth and fled from them naked.

This was the night of Christ's arrest, trial and eventual crucifixion. The disciples were shocked that Christ allowed himself to be apprehended. Their Hero, their Mentor, their Leader and their Friend had just been captured by an angry mob. In an effort to protect themselves, they left their Master and scurried to hiding places like so many roaches when the lights come on.

This is where our next streaker takes the scene. We don't know his name. It seems that he had good intentions. He hadn't forsaken Jesus, not yet anyway, as many of the disciples had. The text says that he was following Him, that is Christ. Perhaps he was too close. Perhaps someone recognized him as a disciple. Whatever the situation, some young men grabbed him. And I am sure that set his adrenaline going. The fight or flight reaction took over.

He knew that because of his association with Jesus he was at risk. And so I can see his legs begin pumping like a running back, trying to shake off his attackers.

His arms are flailing and he's ducking and dodging with more moves than a monkey on a hundred yards of grapevine. And all they get is his clothes as he runs off naked and he is glad to let them have them. Don't you wonder what he told his mother when he got home?

This fellow streaked by choice. What were the motivating factors? There are several.

He was so anxious to disassociate himself with Christ that he ran naked. Evidently the presence of Jesus was so unattractive to him that he would rather be seen naked than to be seen with Christ. It really makes you wonder about your friends. You see, this young man was a follower of Christ. He was an insider. Christ considered him a friend, but when the going got tough, he left. When it got hot in the kitchen, he decided to chill. When Christ needed a friend, he was gone in the wind.

Many of Christ's friends forsook Him that night and I wonder how many are forsaking Him today in order to have a good time. In order to not be seen as too holy, in order to enjoy the pleasures of sin for a season. We call ourselves friends of Christ, but how much time do we spend with this Friend? How much time do we spend building a relationship with our Friend? How well do you know this Friend? And, how well do we want Him to really know us?

This young man preferred nakedness to the presence of Christ. Is there a pet sin, a minor indiscretion, or a peccadillo that we are holding onto that is separating us from God's presence, that is separating us from enjoying a full relationship with Christ? We need to give it up

51

now before it separates us from Christ eternally and then it won't be a secret any more as it will be laid bare before the universe.

He was afraid of what man would do to him. I suppose he had forgotten Christ's admonition not to fear those who can take the body, but those who can take the soul. Fear is a compelling emotion. It can debilitate. It can strangle. It can cripple. It is the greatest source of inaction in the world. Fear is an acronym. It stands for False Evidence Appearing Real. It is the opposite of faith, which is belief that transcends evidence. Faith causes action. Fear causes inaction. We have nothing to fear for the future except that we forget the way the Lord has led us.

This fellow by his actions showed that he was more afraid of man than God. That's because he believed man more than God. People continue to place more stock in the threats of man than the promises of God. That's why they lie, steal, fornicate, withhold tithes and offerings, and debilitate their bodies with drugs and alcohol and an indulgent lifestyle.

Sin is the result of a broken faith relationship. We distrust God's good intentions and His excellent advice and take the word of mortal self-possessed sinners over the One Who loves us best. Think about it. What worlds did they create? What universe do they rule? For what world did they die? For what sinner did they sacrifice? How can we give them God's place in our life?

Our streaker was afraid that people would think he was different so he did something out of the ordinary.

Here he was concerned about how he was perceived by his peers. You see the text says that he was a young man and young men chased him. Everyone is concerned to some degree as to their status, how others perceive them.

Think about it like this. How do you determine who you are? Where do you draw your sense of self-esteem? That is, are you the person that you think you are? Or are you the person others think you are? Or are you the person you think others think you are? Invariably you are the person you think others think you are. Other people have a lot to do in establishing what we think of ourselves. If you are constantly told that you have a particular skill, talent, ability or trait, you will begin to develop that trait. On the most basic level, if you get what you consider to be a bad haircut and everyone compliments you on your haircut, how do you feel about your hair? I know people who will buy something in an exclusive store just to impress the clerk. They will buy something that they don't need to impress somebody that they don't even know. I also know a gentleman who has begun a singing career only because other people told him that he had a good voice. And on the other hand there is a young man who will never play the piano in public because someone who was influential in his life told him that he had no talent. We are impressed with others' impressions of ourselves. So it is not too much of a stretch to imagine that our youthful runner was also.

This young man evidently was finding greater esteem from his youthful friends than he did in his association with Jesus. That's sad. What is sadder is if we are missing the blessings that come from association with Christ because it's not "cool". Let me tell you something. There's coming a time when God's going to take all of the cool people and heat them up.

Along the same lines, he was more concerned about what people thought than what Christ thought. All the time that he had spent in Christ's presence had little influence in his decision to run. I am sure that his actions were instinctive and none of us know what we would do in a moment of pressure. However our initial reactions show what is at our base level.

Finally he was more concerned about himself than Christ. For the past three and a half years Jesus had only lived to serve and help others. Now Christ had just been apprehended by a rude and demon possessed mob. By his action, this streaker was saying like the thief on the cross, "He saved others, let Him save Himself."

It's quite obvious that he was not streaking for Jesus.

Our third example is found in Genesis 39.12

And she caught him by his garment, saying, Lie with me: and he left his garment in her hand and fled, and got him out.

Joseph streaked also. Now I am not sure that he ran away totally naked. But the text says he left his cloak and that will suffice for my illustration.

Sold as a slave by his brothers, living alone in a foreign land he could have easily followed the maxim,

"When in Rome…" Who knew, who would know, who would care?

Joseph knew the answer to that. His response to Mrs. Potipher showed no concern for her, her husband or in fact anyone in all of Egypt. But he said, "How could I do this great sin against God?" And he ran. He left his cloak. Joseph streaked for God.

What were Joseph's motivating factors? How does he differ from the young man in Mark?

- Joseph was more concerned about what God thought about him than what others thought.
- He was more concerned about God than himself.
- He didn't care if people thought that he was different so he did the extraordinary.
- He was so anxious to disassociate himself with sin that he ran.

Joseph's soul thrilled with the high resolve to prove himself true to God – under all circumstances to act as became a subject of the King of Heaven. He would serve the Lord with undivided heart; he would meet the trials of his lot with fortitude and perform every duty with fidelity. One day's experience had been a turning point in Joseph's life. Its terrible calamity had transformed him from a petted child to a man, thoughtful, courageous and self-possessed. He streaked for Jesus. What will it take to make you streak?

Before you get confused I am in no way indicating, suggesting, implying, intimating or indicating in any fashion that you are supposed to run naked and do that for Christ. However, there are two things about streakers that I want you to observe. First they disrobe and second they are exhibitionists.

As followers of Christ we have some things we need to remove so that the light of God's love can be seen in us. We are uptight with pride, position, status, bigotry, materialism, self-centeredness, and the sensuality of the age. We need to shake them off, disrobe so that we can streak, that is, run the race that God has set before us. These are the same qualities that we must lose if we expect to cross Jordan.

We need to get naked. That is strip ourselves of those weights that so easily beset us. Things like pride, position, vanity, self-centeredness, licentiousness, and materialism. We need to bare our souls to the Master and plead for the power of the Holy Spirit otherwise, we will be indistinguishable from the other west side residents.

And we need to be exhibitionists. Not of these naked, sin infected bodies. The irony of today's exhibitionists in contrast with Adam and Eve's perfect bodies is amazing. Our first parents when they discovered that they were naked were ashamed and looked to quickly cover up. After the physical decline of 6,000 years of sin we don't know enough to cover up. Amazing, isn't it? We need to be exhibitionists, all right, exhibits of the power of God, living testimonies for the world.

That's the last thing Satan wants you to do. There is a legend of a king in ancient times that had a beautiful daughter. Young men came from all over the then known world to ask her hand in marriage. To each the king would reply the same. Whoever could beat his daughter in a foot race could win her hand in marriage. And of all of the suitors, not one was her match in running.

There is a legend concerning a young man who arrives from a far country and he says that he has traveled a long way to race and win the young maiden as his bride. As the race begins he and the maiden are running stride for stride. He was indeed a talented athlete, but not a match for the princess because she begins to take a lead. Just as she begins to advance, the challenger removes an object from his clothing and tosses it in front of her. It is a golden apple. It is her favorite fruit in her favorite form. She slows to pick it up. Each time she moves ahead, he tosses another apple. The result is that she loses the race to her new husband. Her outcome was not too bad. It was neither fatal nor eternal. Satan is buying your soul with his own golden apples. The only difference is that they are not even real. They are made of fool's gold!

Satan wants to trade your victor's crown for the pleasures and comfort of this world. You hear many people talking about their comfort zone and what is in it and what isn't. The demands of streaking for Jesus are certainly not within the comfort zones of many Christians or successful Jordan crossers. I wonder where Calvary fit into Christ's comfort zone. I wonder where living for three and a half years in this sin-infected planet fit into His comfort zone. God's call for you today is to come out of that comfort zone. He needs you to streak; because that is the way you will make a difference.

Bigger and better is what you buy
To deafen your ears to the hungry cry
When will you realize that enough is enough?
And strip yourself of material stuff
Streak for Jesus

Dressed in pride position and fame
These are all tokens of the earthly game
Lay them all at the foot of the cross
Despite their sheen they are not but dross
Streak for Jesus

Lay your affections on things above
You spend your time with what you love
In heaven the streets are paved with gold
What is the price placed on your soul?
Streak for Jesus

We are running a race, a race against sin
We have God's assurance that we will win
But we must lay aside every hindering weight
Or else defeat will be our fate
Streak for Jesus

Noah streaked when he built the ark
Moses streaked when he struck the rock
Daniel streaked when he prophesized the end
Jesus streaked when He saved his 3 friends

Mary streaked with a bottle of alabaster

Jonah streaked when he warned of disaster
Enoch streaked and never saw a grave
Jesus streaked and the world was saved

Ezekiel streaked and saw a wheel in a wheel
A little boy streaked and 5,000 had a meal
We need more streakers before we are through
And the world is waiting for a streaker named you

Contrast Joseph and the youth in Mark chapter 15. Their ability to streak was determined by influential others in their lives. The youth in Mark ran naked because he was fearful of what mortal men would think about him and what they would do to him. He had no apparent concern as to what Jesus thought. Consider this, although he was a follower of Christ, Mark did not think enough of him to include his name in the story. Joseph's only interest on the other hand was what God thought concerning him. The thoughts made all of the differences in their actions.

To cross Jordan you will need to reject the enticing influences of the world. Their allurements are deadly. You must cast off, as Paul says, every weight that besets. You might lose some friends. But were they really friends anyway? You might become less popular. But whose opinion really matter? Replace all of that with the heavenly influence of the only One Who really cares about you, the One Who can do exceedingly above all that you ask or think. That is when you will be able to streak. And then I'll see you on the other side.

Chapter 5

Can You Hear Me Now?

In the beginning was the Word… and the Word became flesh and dwelled among us.
John The Beloved

"Opportunities are often missed because we are broad-
casting when we should be listening."
Author Unknown

"If only God would give me some clear sign! Like making a large deposit in my name in a Swiss Bank."
Woody Allen

The Word became flesh; I consider this the pen-
ultimate example of communication. The Word
that spoke creation, the Word that sits at the
right hand of God, the Word that holds the universe and
your heart in His hand, that Word now through transpo-
sition, extrapolation or some type of genetic manipula-
tion becomes flesh. Why? So that we can more clearly
behold the glory of His Father. And He says to you,
"Can you hear Me now?"

God is communicating to us a message of life and
death. Our response to that message determines our
eternity. Unfortunately there are some impediments to
our understanding His message and consequently making the best choice. God's directions for crossing Jordan

will mean little if we don't get the message.

One of my pastimes that brings me the most pleasure is my backyard pond. We (I) dug the hole, covered it with a liner, added water, rocks, a waterfall and landscaping. Trees, shrubs and water plants combine to create a natural looking setting. We (I) added some fish, Japanese koi, to add to my pleasure and the pleasure of my guests.

Koi can be easily domesticated. Many evenings were spent feeding them and watching their colors flash as they responded to the food I provided. They would eat from my hands. In fact, some became so accustomed to me that they would allow me to stroke their sides similarly to the way you would pet a dog or a cat.

The fish flourished in their habitat. All went well until an enemy appeared. My first indication was seeing lily leaves floating on the water having been clipped off of at the stem. It was curious, but I couldn't find a reason for it. My next indication was that the fish seemed more agitated and were not as eager as before to come out for feeding. Then I discovered the perpetrator. A snapping turtle had found a home in the bottom of my pond. Unabated, he would easily decimate my entire pond population.

Something needed to be done. I needed to rescue the fish, but they were even afraid of me. I had provided their habitat. I built it with my own hands. I selected the plants. I designed their eco-system. I even fed them with a special menu. I delighted at their company and now that they were in trouble they treated me as though

I was a total stranger. Their lack of trust was understandable. After all they were just fish. Their ability to comprehend much beyond their existence was minimal.

Suddenly I was overtaken by an epiphany. Wouldn't it be a wonderful thing for me to become a fish so that I could explain to them in fish talk just what I am all about and how I want to save them? Just as quickly as I got that epiphany reality testing got the best of me. I liked the fish, but not that much. Why would I ever want to leave the comfort of my home and wife and family and friends for the limited world of a backyard pond? Do I desire muck in my life? Do I prefer eating algae and fish food to apple pie and ice cream? What part of "saving the fish" will improve anything that I have going on right now? Worst-case scenario, I get rid of the snapper and replenish the pond with new fish, because they're just fish, right?

If you haven't guessed by now, my pond dilemma parallels in an imperfect way the decision of divinity in sending Christ, the Word, to become flesh. It was to communicate eternal truths to a temporal society. The only way it could be effected was by clothing the incarnate with carnal, the immortal with immortality.

Communication is complex on any level. Even though we participate in some type of interaction on a daily basis, we pay little attention to its machinations. Marshall McLuhan stated that the medium is the message. That's why messengers get shot. But that's also why the Word had to become flesh. McLuhan's statement promotes the power of the medium to shape the message to a point that the two become indistinguishable. Consider the message to be water and its medium, the container of the message, a Clorox bleach bottle. If I were to offer you water poured from a bleach bottle, I doubt you would drink it regardless of your thirst. You very validly interpret the function of the water based on its container. In a similar manner we conjoin message and media into a cohesive unit.

All communication relies on coding and decoding. Before you speak you usually think about what you want to say and consider how to relay it to your audience. You might give the same message to a six year old and a sixty year old, but the way you encode it for your intended audience is a skill you use for effective communication. Just as you encode, you also have to decode the messages you receive. That is where communication issues begin.

Because of our various backgrounds we tend to listen with a personal bias, some people call it spin, as a result the message we think we heard may not have been what was said because of our listening filters. What follows are some different types of listeners and their decoding issues.

Emotional listeners

*"And, lo thou art unto them as a very lovely song of one that hath a pleasant voice, and can play well on an instrument: for they hear the words, **but they do them not.**"*
Ezekiel 33:32

These are people who hear the message, perhaps in a song or sermon, but it has no power in their life. They will tell you the sermon was great but can't tell you what it was about. They sing, "Here am I send me" and refuse to hold office one, or if a neighbor calls, they are too busy. They are so caught up with the external that they can't see the eternal.

There was a television show in the sixties called Medic. From what I understand it was a popular show. It had good ratings. The show was cancelled. And the reason was that the program was so compelling watchers ignored the commercials. They heard the words but didn't buy one product.

This group of listeners is so consumed with pomp that they have no awareness of their circumstance. Hear the words but do not do them. Like James Brown says, they're talking loud and saying nothing. Their life shows no evidence of being with Christ. But Christ says to them, "Can you hear Me now?"

Foolish Listeners

And everyone that heareth these sayings of mine, and doeth them not, shall be likened unto the foolish man which built his house on the sand. Matt 7.26

These are people that hear and don't do. They are the ones that ignore the obvious. You see them in school. The teacher says that there will be a test on Friday. Do they study? No, they're foolish. They hear and don't do. They live only for today and don't believe in a judgment. Even the devils believe. They think they can charm themselves out of every predicament, because they are smarter than everyone. (That's the way fools think). A teacher told me about an occasion that underscores this principle. She was responsible for the stage crew for a school production. In order to encourage all of the children, she selected a student to assist her who had some outstanding character struggles. Midway through the production the audience is shocked to witness a single fist with a single finger emerge from behind the curtain. The teacher grabbed the offending finger and the connected hand and pulled the coupled body from behind the curtain. His defense, "It wasn't me." But even to him and all like him Christ says, "Can you hear Me, Now?"

Superficial listeners

When any one heareth the word of the kingdom and understandeth it not, then cometh the wicked one, and catcheth away that which was sown in his heart. This is he which recieveth the seed by the wayside. Matthew 13:19

The next group is shallow according to Matthew 13.19. These people are easily led, naïve, they believe everything and question nothing. They can tell you thousands of things that are in the Bible, but have never read it for themselves. They follow every new light; they are not grounded because they don't know the truth or God's voice. They are hypocrites. And they come in two categories; those who are deceitful and dishonest to others and those who are deceitful and dishonest to themselves. That's a dangerous place to be, as genuine as natural vinyl. That's Laodicea. Can you hear Me now?

The best way I can describe this next group is hard headed –

And He said unto him, If they hear not Moses and the prophets, neither will they be persuaded, though one rose from the dead. (Luke 16.31)

Now, you know what they say about a hard head? Jesus told them that they wouldn't even believe Moses if he rose from the dead. It's because they believe in themselves more than anyone else. I saw a bumper sticker that best describes them "Those people who think they know everything are annoying to those of us who do." They are inflexible, cynical and negative and they refuse to listen except to when you are taking a breath so that they can get their two cents in. They can tell you everything that won't work. Now they do have ideas about what will work, but they also have a reason why someone else won't let them do what they see needs to be done. Eager to speak, they think that they know what you're about to say and as a result won't let you say anything. A real waste of time, but God says, "Can you hear Me now?"

Absentminded hearers

For if any be a hearer of the word, and not a doer, he is like unto a man beholding his natural face in a glass: For he beholdeth himself, and goeth his way, and straightway forgetteth what manner of man he was. James 1.23,24

These aren't what we euphemistically refer to as senior moments. Everyone says absentmindedness or forgetfulness is a sign of old age. Kids forget, too. They just don't worry about it as much as adults do. This situation is more than in one ear and out the other. Why? It is because these hearers don't care. People remember what matters. The more important it is the easier it is to remember. How often do you have to remind your children to do chores? How often do you have to remind them to get an extra cookie, sleep late or play video games? It is obvious we remember what is important. Can you hear Me now?

These hearers of the word are putting in face time but not ear time. Listening is probably one of the most difficult of all of the communication skills. It requires patience and the desire to process what is being heard. All too frequently, those on the listening side are merely listening for a break in the conversation so that they can interject whatever it is that is on their mind. Consequently the quality of the communication is sacrificed to the agenda of the egocentric hearer. Can you hear Me now?

Regardless, God is the ultimate communicator. He

67

doesn't give up trying to reach humanity. Rev 3.30 I stand at the door and knock – Can You hear Me now?

Through other media He tries to get His message through. Can you hear Me now?

He sent a donkey to Balaam, a burning bush to Moses.
To Abraham it was a ram in the thicket.
To Jacob it was a ladder.
To Paul it was his infirmity.
To Rahab it was a red chord.
To Peter it was a rooster.
To Noah it was a rainbow.
To David it was a second chance.
To Job it was affliction.
To shepherds it was an angel chorus.
To Hosea it was an adulterous wife.
To Ezekiel it was a wheel in a wheel.
To Thomas it was a touch.
To the woman taken in adultery it was silence.
To Zacchaeus it was a dinner guest.
To the thief on the cross it was a promise.

He has sent prophets and will send prophets.

Joel 2:28 And it shall come to pass afterward that I shall pour out my spirit upon all flesh and your sons and your daughters shall prophesy and your old men shall dream dreams and your young men shall see visions.
Can you hear Me now?
He is revealed in nature. There are sermons in stones.

68

Miracles occur daily within our view. The seven-day cycle is evidence of Creation. All of our time from milliseconds to centuries is based on something astronomical. The only exception to that is the seven-day week. It is based on the creative power of God. And it has been that way, just because He said so.

Another amazing revelation of God's creative genius displayed in nature is the fact that water freezes and expands. You say, "Big deal." Well, it is a big deal. Everything in nature contracts when it freezes. Water is the only exception. If water contracted like all other substances, it would sink to the bottom rather than float. That would keep your ice in the bottom of your glass. But more importantly, all ice would sink to the bottom of lakes and rivers eventually causing them to become solid block of ice. Can you hear Me now?

He is speaking to us through signs in the sky. Astronomers will tell you that all of the planets are lining up in what they call a conjunction and they realize that something of cosmic importance is about to take place. Far out in space, light years behind the Great Nebula and the Pleiades there's a great stirring and rush of excitement beyond human description. One can hear chariots rumble. Thunder rolls like kettledrums and lightening shakes is fiery white lances. The trumpets sound. He's on His way!! Can you hear Me now?

I'm talking about the coming of the Word.

He is the earth's Creator, the soul saver, the request

receiver, the pain reliever,
    He is the new heart maker, the burden taker, the hair counter, the true fountain,
    He is a warm cover, a true lover, a friend to the end, the one who'll defend
    He is Jacob's ladder, the joy adder, the tear gatherer.
The pain sharer, He is the Word,
    The Word that existed before time

    Before there was anything, there was the Word,
    The omnipotent, omniscient, magnificent Word

    Defined by infinity, filled with divinity, sent by the trinity, The Word

    Witness in creation, the loving revelation and the only explanation is the Word

    Through heavens portal, the immortal became mortal, made in flesh, the Word

    But people refused Him, wrongfully accused Him, unmercifully abused Him, the Word

    Though people profane Him, it is love that sustains Him as His Father reclaims Him, the Word

    I'm talking about Jesus He's the Word
    And He will not be deterred
    He's the best news this world has ever heard

Anything else is just absurd
Speaking out to rich and poor
I'm still knocking at the door
Knocking as loud at the law will allow
I want to know can you hear me now?

What's standing in the way of your hearing the Master's voice? Is it that you are making too much noise? Be Still, God says, "and know that I am God." Knowledge of God is not found in busyness but in stillness. It is then we can hear His still small voice and He's saying;

"This is the way walk ye in it." Isaiah 30:29
"Take no thought how or what ye shall speak; for it shall be given you in that same hour what ye shall speak." Matthew 10:19
"For I will give you a mouth and wisdom which all your adversaries shall not be able to gainsay or resist." Luke 21:15
"The Lord hath given me the tongue of the learned that I should know how to speak a word in season to him that is weary." Isaiah 50:4

The result is that we become the medium through which God speaks to others. You reflect God's character, because you have become like God. What an awesome privilege and responsibility! This is the goal of life, which is merely accomplished by listening to the Master.

Our lifestyle and orientation parallel the church of Laodicea (Revelation 3: 14-22). His appeal to this church is I stand at the door and knock. Can you hear Me now? What more can He do or say to get the message through? At some point we've got to take the responsibility to turn down the music, turn off the TV, turn off the distractions and cut the static. We have to become listeners rather than hearers.

God is speaking to you today. Are you listening? Can you hear Him now? He'll be calling you tomorrow. Will you be available? Take time to listen to His appeal and I'll meet you on the other side.

Chapter 6

A Healthy Body

Your health is your only wealth.
Anonymous

Beloved, I wish above all things that thou mayest prosper and be in health.
III John 3:2

The weaker the body, the more it commands. The stronger the body, the more it obeys.
Calvin Lester

"As I see it, every day you do one of two things; build health or produce disease in yourself."
Adelle Davis

Recent research gives evidence to the effect of lifestyle issues on our health. Just watch television for any amount of time and you will see that America is obsessed with addressing a broad assortment of health matters. Bald heads, obesity, acid reflux, Human Pap Loma Virus, high cholesterol, bad breath, athletes' foot, sun burn, weak bladders, love handles, cavities, cramps, yellow teeth, sexual dysfunction, chronic back pain, allergies, the common cold and a variety of other ailments may find their nemesis on commercial television. Based on what I have seen, health is big business.

People are beginning to realize that a price is to be paid for a healthy body. Some pay the price early and reap dividends later. Others, unwilling to pay the price early, only have the option of paying later. Unfortunately, then the price they pay is much higher.

If you would be successful in crossing Jordan, a healthy body is a valuable asset. In this chapter we will talk about the importance of maintaining a healthy body.

One of the reasons for maintaining a healthy body is in the Calvin Lester quotation above. Calvin Lester is a Christian man who has several extremely dark belts in martial arts. Calvin came to this conclusion as a result of his training. He shared the thought with me as a reminder as to the effects of physical weakness. Simply stated, the weaker our bodies are, the greater is our bodies' demand for control. For example, weak bodies want to stay in bed longer, eat whenever and whatever they want and they are likely to be less temperate. Strong bodies also want to sleep late, eat whenever and whatever they want and have intemperate inclinations. The critical difference here is that the stronger bodies are obedient to the mind whereas the weaker bodies challenge the mind for control of whatever decisions are made.

To see how this plays out imagine that it is six o'clock in the morning. You have reset your alarm twice already and you realize that you made a commitment to yourself to run three miles every morning. Your resolution is challenged by the howl of the wind as rain splashes against your window. The weak body encourages you to maintain your resolve to exercise but just not now. Sometime later in the week when the sun is shining would be better. By contrast the stronger body moves to complete the unfavorable action with the assent of the mind realizing that this is the better choice.

One man shared with me what he did when facing a similar decision. Knowing that he should exercise, realizing that he did not want to exercise, he said he prayed for strength. What he said happened next was marvelous. He said that the Lord did not give him the requested power to affirm his resolve. Instead he said he was blessed with wisdom and as a result he turned over and went back to sleep!

The weaker body doesn't know how to say no (except to anything which will challenge the status quo). So you eat the extra piece of cake, dismiss your exercise routine, imbibe, satiate, indulge, compromise, rationalize and settle for the path of least resistance. Weaker bodies have difficulty with delayed gratification. There may be even a mental awareness that the option chosen is a poor choice. It is the pull of the weak physical nature that overrules all wisdom.

This phenomenon was displayed in rather dramatic fashion in a consult that I was doing with a fourteen-year-old young man. We were looking at his current choices and examining their long-term effects. He enjoyed what he was doing, much to his detriment. His method of reconciling his behavior with the inevitable result was to state that he agreed that he was messing up his life. So he figured that when he turned thirty or forty it would be so messed up that he would just commit suicide. His example though rare, I hope, speaks volumes to our capacity for self-destruction. That's the reason, Jesus chided his disciples that night prior to His crucifixion with the statement, "The spirit is willing, but the flesh is weak."

Christ had asked his closest friends to pray with Him as He prepared for what would be the most grueling challenge any human would ever confront. He found them sleeping each time he returned to them. He acknowledged to them the power of weak flesh to overrule the best of intentions. What Christ spoke to them that night was more than just a patronizing statement. He was telling them and us that desire without action is meaningless. Hear Him saying, "I know you want to stay up and pray, but I know you can't because you're weak." He says to us, "I know you want to cross Jordan, but you can't because you're weak" All of your desire without action mean little, because your result has the same effect as the person who never even tried.

The Apostle Paul knew this dilemma. In his classic soliloquy of introspection that is Romans 7, he shares the anguish of his frustration. Caught between the "wants" and the "shoulds," Paul searches for peace to reconcile his spirit. Only when he recognizes the power of God in his infirmity does he receive satisfaction and rejoice in a new understanding.

A submitted will is the beginning of any campaign. Christ on the eve of His passion prayed that the Father's will would supercede His own. Our success in crossing Jordan is not based on efficient stratagem and implementation. Rather, it is wholly centered on our acceptance of the will of God in our life. Now you say, what does all of that have to do with being healthy?

John answers succinctly, "Beloved," he says. "I wish above all things that you prosper and be in health, even as thy soul prospereth." John equates our physical health to our spiritual health. His assertion is accurately based. Because we are physical creatures, most of our influences are experienced physically. Health and spirituality possess weighty power over each other.

Additionally our bodies are temples for the Most High. We have the responsibility of being stewards of these fleshy temples. "What? Know ye not that your body is the temple of the Holy Ghost which is in you, which ye have of God, and ye are not your own? 1Corinthians 6:19. It has always been my practice to use an extra level of care whenever I am using an item that belongs to someone else. I had borrowed a mower because mine was broken. And instead of running over the branches and stones like I might have with mine (perhaps that's why mine was broken) I exercised greater caution in those areas. My plan was to return it in better shape than I had gotten it. I wanted the loaner of the mower to be pleased that he had allowed me the opportunity to use his mower. We are commissioned by heaven to look after these bodies. They are not ours. We want the Creator to be pleased that He placed them in our care.

Furthermore we were created in the image of God. It is our responsibility to reflect the character of God to others. It is difficult to reflect Divinity in a body that is indulgent and undisciplined. This is a classic example of the medium being the message. And what message does an intemperate body convey?

God will bless us as we do His will. He will empower us as we follow His biddings. And because He is God, He can complete His will using whatever type of instrumentality He desires. However, it is also obvious that it is easier to work with a sharp ax than a dull one. A tuned automobile is the preferred option to its poorly running counterpart. A healthy body will adequately reflect its Creator, it will not lead you into temptation and it will accept the challenge of your quest in crossing Jordan.

I hope you prosper and be in health. And I'll see you on the other side.

Chapter 7

Perseverance

There is no failure except in no longer trying. There is
no defeat except from within, no really insurmountable
barrier save our own inherent weakness of purpose.
Kin Hubbard

"But this one thing I do, forgetting those things which
are behind, and reaching forth unto those things which
are before, I press toward the mark for the prize of the
high calling of God in Christ Jesus."
Philippians 4:13, 14

The probability that we might fail in the struggle ought
not to deter us from the support of a cause we believe
to be just.
Abraham Lincoln

The Difficult is that which can be done immediately,
the Impossible that which takes a little longer.
George Santayana

When the going gets tough, say God and I are enough.
Sam Darby

Some call it stick-to-itiveness, others persistence.
We will call it perseverance. Regardless of the
name the qualities of the characteristics are identi-
cal. It is that postage stamp quality. That is the ability to

stick to the job until the job is done. Potentially, this trait can be the determinant for the side of Jordan on which you will reside.

So many have dreams, goals and desires that lay in a clump of disinterest like yesterday's newspaper. The fire of hope extinguished by the frustration of obstacles perceived insurmountable, of vision stealing friends and associates and of the comfort of the status quos. The frustration is real as are all of roadblocks. But if they had the potency that we ascribe to them, none would succeed. Everyone would live on Jordan's west side. However if one pilgrim can pass through the vale of doubt and fear, you can too. If you persevere you can win! Doctoral students are told that this terminal degree is not awarded to necessarily the brightest students, but to those who persist and persevere to achieve their goal. Perseverance is a quality of character ascribed not on the basis of intellect, race, creed, socio-economic status, age, gender, height, weight, religion, nationality or skin color. Its accessibility makes it the perfect addition to any personal growth agenda.

What follow are some suggestions to assist you in becoming the persevering persistent pilgrim that will cross your Jordan River.

Have A Goal

It is impossible to persevere if you do not have a goal or know where you are going. If you have no goal, you are like the couple headed down the highway just as lost as they can be. The wife, with her native navigational system, informs the husband that they are lost. And to his credit he acknowledges her assessment of the situation as correct, but his rejoinder is that she should be pleased because they are making great time. His perseverance without a meaningful goal is pretty useless and it takes redundancy to a whole new level.

The point then is to have a goal. One is good. More is better. Highly meaningful is much better. Israel wanted to cross the Jordan to be free, to have their own lands, to have vineyards and farms, and to build a future for their progeny. What is it that you want that only crossing your Jordan can give you? How desperately do you desire it? How different would your life be if you attained that goal? What would life be like for you if your goal were not reached? Consider these questions as you formulate the cause for your campaign, the point for which you will persevere. Without a significantly passionate purpose you may as well find housing on Jordan's west bank. You can't leave home without it.

Value your Goal

Equally important to having a goal is the way you treat it. Mistreated goals are devalued and rendered ineffective. The following anecdote should explain what I mean. I was in a workshop and a participant shared this experience. She happened to be in an airport in Tokyo, Japan. While waiting for her flight, she noticed a rather well dressed older gentleman who seemed preoccupied with something in his hands. It appeared to her that he had some prayer beads or something similar. Since she is always interested in things spiritual, she engaged him in conversation. She was surprised to discover that he was the President of Sony Corporation. Her level of surprise increased when she found out what was consuming his attention. He was not involved in meditation, at least in the traditional sense. Instead he was reviewing his personal goals, short term and long term.

It is no secret that success is linked to our treatment of our goals. Research with Harvard graduates revealed that those who wrote out their goals and reviewed them daily were more successful than their counterparts who had goals but were satisfied to have them in their head. This is what I was referring to concerning your goal treatment. The best way to make your goal work for you is to give yourself regular reminders of what you are aiming for. I have pictures on my wall of the cars I want to buy and of the house I want to build. I have visuals for the charities I want to support. You have to work at reminding yourself of your goal. It is important for you to do if you are serious about crossing Jordan and it is nobody else's responsibility but yours.

Moses had the right idea when it came to reminding Israel about their goals. He outlines the procedure rather clearly in Deuteronomy 6:6-9. It says

And these words, which I command thee this day, shall be in you heart: And thou shalt teach them diligently to thy children, and shalt talk of them when thou sittest in thine

house, and when thou walkest in the way, and when thou liest down, and when thou risest up. And thou shalt bind them for a sign upon thine hand, and they shall be as frontlets between thine eyes. And thou shalt write them upon the posts of thy house, and on thy gates.

You should understand that Moses thought these tenets were extremely important to remember. If you have some goals for crossing Jordan you need to treat them the same way. Put pictures, signs and messages all around your home to remind you of your goals. One lady put a picture of a woman that was her ideal, in terms of size and weight, on her refrigerator. Every time she went to the fridge, the image reminded her of her goal and deterred her from excess eating. She noticed though a side effect of her stratagem. Her husband, conversely, was spending more time at the refrigerator!

Well-set goals will assist you in persevering. They are obstacle over comers. As you cross your Jordan you will encounter obstructions to your progress. The greater the goal, the greater the roadblock. As you hit that seemingly insurmountable delay to your crossing, you start to doubt your resolve. You wonder why you started this thing in the first place. You could be somewhere "chilling" like everybody else. But before you go back to Egypt or even settle for the west side, take a moment to reflect on the why. That's your goal. What was the compelling reason to begin with? If you have a good reason, a good reason is one that gives you goose bumps, you will be able to look past the current inconveniences and visualize your completed campaign.

Visualize your Goal

Visualization is an under appreciated skill. Athletes, as a part of their preparation spend time visualizing their event. They mentally process every aspect of the contest. They consider the weather, what they are wearing, the crowd noise, and how the event will proceed. Public speakers and other performers follow a similar procedure. I am suggesting that you begin to visualize what it will be like when you achieve your goal.

I recall one summer that I was working on my swimming pool. As the project ensued, it grew much larger that I had anticipated. Walls were collapsing. I needed a new pump and filter. The water seemingly refused to maintain any type of clarity. Despite all of that, the vision of relaxing in the cool of the pool in the privacy of my home was the only thing that encouraged me to persevere rather than to close it up and purchase a membership to the local swim club. I envisioned myself floating aimlessly in the summer sun. I pictured a July 4th cookout and a game of volleyball in the water. I even contemplated, in imagination, some moon light swimming wearing nothing but a smile which, I understand, was not permitted by my local swim club. That might make a disturbing mental image for you, but it is just the visual that I needed.

Have a Support Team

In addition to your goal you should have a support

team. Anyone who does anything of any magnitude has a support team. Be it running for President, climbing Mount Everest, walking on the moon, having a baby, or graduating from high school, you need a support team. If you want to expedite your crossing, if you want to facilitate your persevering, you will also need a support team. Your team is constructed of two types of people. One group is allies. The other group is mentors.

The allies are your friends. They are people who agree with your philosophy. They may also have a Jordan to cross. So by your regular interaction, you build each other up. Meeting with your allies is important. Through mutual edification you are encouraged to share your goals and process your progress. Your allies create a safe place for positive growth as opposed to the dream stealers who, like their name, wish to steal your dream right from out of your heart. Just as allies should be cultivated, dream stealers should be avoided. The impact of either group on your campaign is quite compelling.

Mentors compose the second part of your support team. They are people who have done what it is you want to do. If what you want to do is so unique no one has done it, then they are the people with the information and experience that you lack. Seek them out and gain their expertise. In most cases they will be glad to offer you assistance. It gives validity to their know-how. They can share the pitfalls and short cuts. The wheel need only be invented once.

Embrace Failure

There is one other aspect of persistence that should be addressed. That is the possibility of failure. Many fear failure so much that they refuse to act because of the potential for failure. The lack of understanding about failure caused many to shrink from challenge for fear of the stigma, castigation and shame that they erroneously associate with failing. Failure is not an event. It is a decision. Regardless of how many times you miss the mark, you haven't failed until you assent to defeat.

Too many erroneously avoid failure. It is probably out of a lack of understanding of what it really is. Too many psyches are threatened by the idea that they might have failed at anything. The problem with this mentality is that by not risking failure, they are denying themselves the opportunity to grow. Would you have learned to walk if you were afraid of falling? Would we have the light bulb if Thomas Edison ceased trying with his first failed filament? Would anyone know who Colonel Sanders was if he accepted the first rejection of his original recipe? Would we have the magic of Disney Land and Disney World if Walt accepted his firing as an indication that he was not intended to work with cartoons?

Lenny Wilkins is renowned for having more wins than any coach in basketball. He also has the record for losing the most games. Does that make him a failure? Reggie Jackson is in Baseball's Hall of Fame as one of the top ten home run hitters of all time. Reggie also led the league in strikeouts (he's not a pitcher). Does that make him a failure? If you are going to win games, you will lose some in the process. If you are going to hit home runs, there will be sometimes that you will strike out. If you are crossing Jordan, you may not make it on the first try. You may not even make it on the second or third. There is a lesson in every set back; only those who persevere will get it.

The Jordan crosser who perseveres is the one who sets a meaningful goal and is undaunted in its pursuit. If you can visualize the acquisition of your goal in spite of frustrated agendas and daily obstacles, then I guarantee that I will see you on the other side.

Chapter 8
On the Other Side

"Success is all it's cracked up to be."
Daniel Travanti

"The best way to make your dreams come true is to
wake up."
Paul Valery

Cast thy bread upon the waters: for thou shalt find it
after many days.
Ecclesiastes 11:1

The other side of Jordan is where your reward lies. After the rigors of your campaign, you may bask in the sweet satisfaction of succeeded. Despite the frustration, the negative talkers and numerous disappointments, you have accomplished. And for some reason, once you are on the other side, those things just don't seem as intimidating as when they first loomed in your vision on the west side of Jordan.

On the east side you have a new crowd. Those you see welcome you to your success with genuine admiration. They know the trial you endured, because it was theirs also. The mutual level of respect that you experience from like-minded people is refreshing and encouraging.

You enjoy the exhilarating quality of the life of an east side resident. You had assumed that once Jordan was crossed, there would be little left to do. Much to the contrary, east side residents are embarking on new enterprises daily. They regularly cross to the west side to encourage other crossers. In addition they set new standards for themselves. You might call them new Jordan Rivers to cross.

You stand on the bank of the river whose crossing seemed so formidable and realize how much you have grown in the process. You have attained new skills. You have enhanced your gifts. You also have the gratification of goal completion. You had doubted this eventuality. Now that the process is complete take your lessons and share. That is our purpose in life. Then find another river, another mountain, another "Jordan" to cross. You see, the satisfaction in life comes from the journey. So keep crossing and we will get together on the other side.

Discussion Guide

And

Workbook

Introduction

1. What are the benefits of maintaining the status quo and staying inside your comfort zone?
2. What are the benefits of bucking the status quo and moving out of your comfort zone?
3. What is the process that you use for decision-making?
4. Is the process working for you? How do you know?
5. To what degree is fear a factor in your decision-making?
6. How do you see fear or worry as a factor in your faith relationship with God?
7. What are your "giants" and "unassailable walled cities"? How do you deal with them?
8. What decisions would you make if you were guaranteed that you would be successful?
9. Thinking about Caleb and Joshua, have you ever had a time when you went against the majority? What was the issue? What did you learn from the experience?
10. Is there a decision that you made that you would like to do over? What have you learned from that?
11. Are there decisions like Frost's two paths in the woods that have been the best choice for your life? What have you learned from that?
12. What are the things that test your faith? What is the best way to address them?
13. How would your life change if you were addicted to omnipotence?

14. Christ has promised us victory. Make a list of His promises that will encourage you.

_____

_____

_____

_____

15. Read Hebrews 11 and James 2:18,19

Chapter 1 What We Don't Know That We Don't Know

1. Make a list of the blessings that you take for granted. Examples might be; waking up every day, friends, freedom, fresh air, and safety. You may need additional space.

_____

_____

_____

2. What are the things that you trust?

_____

_____

_____

_____

3. List ways that you can go NUTS.

_____

_____

_____

4. What are the "french-fries" in your life? Make a plan to address them. Consider the impact of allowing the Holy Ghost to have His way in your life.
5. Read Deuteronomy 30:19, 20 and James 1:8.

Chapter 2 The Belly of the Beast

1. Are you comfortable with the "lying vanities" in you life?
2. How might you determine if there are some that exist?
3. In what way do you use avoidance?
4. In what way do you use denial?
5. In what way do you use projection?
6. In what way do you use rationalization?
7. Are these behaviors working for you?
8. Are they helping you achieve your goals?
9. Is there something that you can do that would be more effective?
10. In what way can you replace avoidance with assertiveness?
11. In what way can you replace denial with acknowledgement of personal responsibility?
12. In what way can you replace projection with an honest assessment of self?
13. In what way can you replace rationalize (rational lies) with the truth?
14. Are there other "lying vanities" that are in the way of your success?

15. Make a plan to overcome. Use prayer God wants to help.
16. Read James 5:16.

Chapter 3 Stinking Thinking

1. Make a list of all your blessings. Include everything, even the items which are normally taken for granted. Refer to your list from Chapter 1 for help. You may need additional space.

    _____
    _____
    _____

2. Remind yourself regularly that you are indeed blessed of the Lord and highly favored.
3. You are a part of a special creation. Read Psalm 8
4. Personalize your favorite texts. For example; John 3:16 says "For God so loved _____ that He gave His only begotten Son that _____ believes upon Him is saved."
5. Memorize and repeat them over and over.
6. Find some music that encourages you. Gospel themes can be found in all types of music. Identify the genre that best resonates with you and gives you those positive messages and listen often.
7. The more we dwell on negative subjects, the more we breathe life into them. And they become a physical and emotional drain on us. Resolve to breathe life into only positive subjects.

8. Redirect your attention and the attention of whomever you are speaking to to solve the problem rather than rehashing its history.
9. Replace complaining with praise.
10. Thank God for every problem you experience. Read 1 Thessalonians 5:18.
11. Focus your activity on addressing the needs of others. Some suggestions might be to volunteer in a hospital, homeless shelter or women's shelter. Big Brothers and Big Sisters are always looking for "Bigs." Maybe you can assist an elderly person by getting groceries or maybe helping young parents by babysitting and letting them have a night off. There are endless possibilities. Being active in this fashion places the focus outward and helping someone else is a boost to the self-esteem.
12. Read Psalm 118:6.

Chapter 4 Streak for Jesus

1. How often are you motivated by;
   - Fear
   - Power
   - Belonging
   - Friendship
   - Pride
   - What others think
   - What you think that others think
   - What others need

2. List items that you would go out of your comfort zone (sell out) to protect or support regardless of what other people might think about you.

_____

_____

_____

3. Read 1 Samuel 16.7

Chapter 5 Can You Hear Me Now?

1. Read Psalm 19:1-4. To what degree does nature assist us in discovering God?
2. Is the revelation of God through nature complete? Or is there more to God than nature displays?
3. What evidence can you find in nature to support the theory of intelligent design?
4. The phrase "sermons in stones" refers to the concept that nature preaches the gospel. Spend some time organizing your own sermon based upon your observation of the natural world.
5. A story was told of a man who lived in the country stopping a gentleman while at a bus stop to inquire if he also heard the song of a cricket nearby. The gentleman politely noted that in such a busy thoroughfare a sound so minor by comparison could not be heard, let alone be appreciated. Just then someone dropped a quarter on the sidewalk and everybody stopped. We listen for what matters most. How often do we recognize God's "still small voice"?

6. What are the distractions in your life that interfere with you hearing God's voice or witnessing His revelation in nature?
7. How do you make decisions relative to right and wrong? What role does your conscience play in these decisions? How trustworthy is your conscience?
8. What is the value you place on Bible study? Where does it rank with your other activities?
9. In Revelation 3:20, God says, "I stand at the door and knock" demonstrating His eagerness to have a relationship with you. What can you do on a daily basis to improve your relationship with Him?
10. Read John 1:1-17

Chapter 6 – A Healthy Body

1. Solomon advises in Proverbs that a merry heart is like medicine. The suggestion is that a positive outlook on life will prolong a positive lifestyle. Stress is the antagonist to a healthy life. Identify those stress factors and turn them over to Jesus. Christian counselors or therapists are helpful in dealing with stress matters. Read Matthew 11:27-30.
2. Lifestyle issues are the cause of the majority of health problems in the Western society. Items like regular exercise, proper rest and water intake, and a basic diet, if incorporated into one's daily regimen would drastically minimize many doctor visits and hospitalizations. For more information on this subject visit www.newstartliving.com.

3. Read 3 John 1:2

Chapter 7 – Perseverance

1. Consult with the Lord as to what should be your goals. Consider Chapter 5 in understanding His will for you.
2. Review your goal. Write it down. Look at it everyday
3. Visualize yourself in your goal. For example, if you goal is a new job, visualize you parking, what you are driving, what you are wearing, your work environment, your daily duties and so forth.
4. Find people who will encourage and support your goal. This might take you away from some of your best "friends," but it is more important to have positive encouragement when working on goal development.
5. Find someone who went the way before you and ask for guidance. In most cases they will be glad to assist you.
6. Discard Plan B. There is only Plan A. If there is one plan you must commit to it. Plan A burns the boats, the bridge and any other vestige of retreat. That is the way to give true dedication to your goal.
7. Read Philippians 3:13,14

On the Other Side

1. Considering the journey of your life, list below significant milestones in your passage. Births, marriages, graduations and deaths are the usual items we record. In addition to those events, consider chronicling markers such as when you gave your heart to the Lord, when you began to make decisions for yourself or instances when you saw God leading in your life.

    _____
    _____
    _____
    _____
    _____
    _____

2. Make a list of ways that you might assist someone else in accomplishing their goals.

    _____
    _____
    _____
    _____
    _____
    _____

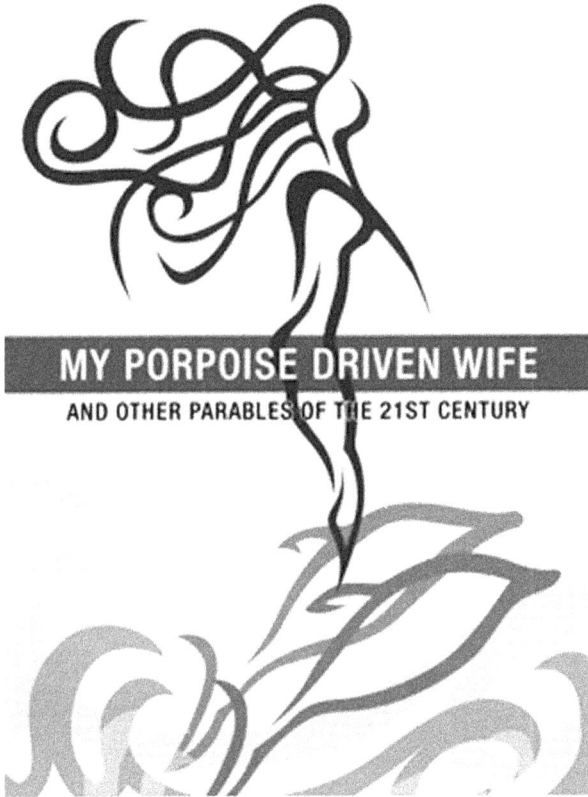

MY PORPOISE DRIVEN WIFE

AND OTHER PARABLES OF THE 21ST CENTURY

Another book by this author is My Porpoise Driven Wife and Other Parables of the 21st Century. This collection of original parables receives acclaim for sharing the aspects of God's Kingdom in contemporary terms. This book is available at KarynnPress.com. Come to the website for FREE offers and other information to improve your Christian walk.